ABOUT THE AUTHOR

Jack Challoner studied physics at Imperial College, London, before training as a science and mathematics teacher. He maintains an active interest in education, dividing his time between the London Science Museum Education Unit and writing science books for children. Mr. Challoner is also an accomplished jazz singer and musician.

Project Editor Laura Buller
Editor Bridget Hopkinson
Art Editor Earl Neish
Production Catherine Semark
Photography Dave King

Library of Congress Cataloging-in-Publication Data
Challoner, Jack.
The science book of numbers/Jack Challoner.—1st U.S. ed.
p.   cm.
"Gulliver books."
Summary: Includes simple activities that illustrate some of the ways we use numbers.
ISBN 0-15-200623-0
1. Numeration—Juvenile literature. 2. Counting—Juvenile literature. [1. Number systems. 2. Counting. 3. Mathematical recreations.]   I. Title.
QA141.C43   1992
513.2'11—dc20   92-3415

Reproduced in Hong Kong by Bright Arts
Printed in Belgium by Proost
First U.S. edition 1992
A B C D E

93.565

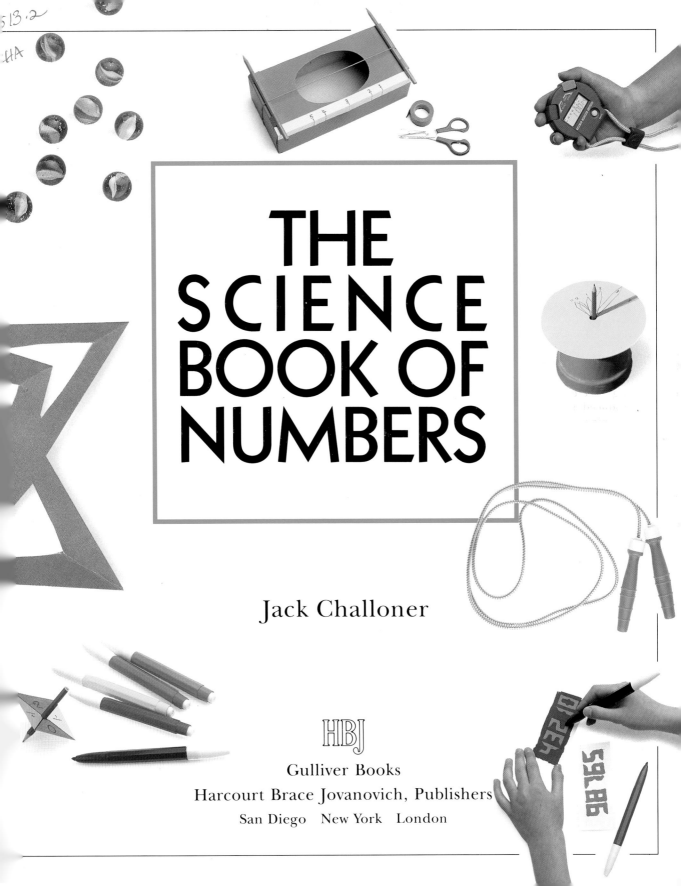

THE SCIENCE BOOK OF NUMBERS

Jack Challoner

HBJ

Gulliver Books

Harcourt Brace Jovanovich, Publishers

San Diego   New York   London

What are numbers?

We use numbers not only to tell "how many," but also "how old," "how far," "how big"—whenever we need to express the exact size or amount of a thing. Without numbers, you could not tell the time, phone your friends, or count your money. You could not keep score in a baseball game or quickly find a page in a book. Numbers help us describe our world.

Helping hands
Our number system is based on groups of ten. This may be because when people first started to count, they used their ten fingers to help them.

Identity tag
Numbers can identify things—almost like giving them names. This penguin wears a tag with its own number so that scientists can recognize it.

Happy birthday
Without numbers, you wouldn't know how old you are or how many candles to put on your birthday cake!

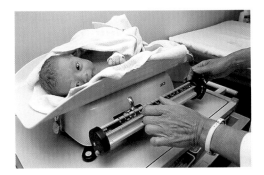

Facts in numbers
Numbers are used to record information about people, too. This newborn baby is being weighed to start a record of her growth.

Jump to it
When you skip, your heart beats faster. Measuring how many times your heart beats per minute is just one way that doctors use numbers.

Two by two
Computers use numbers to perform tasks. The number system computers use is based on twos, instead of tens. It is called the "binary" system.

⚠ This is a warning symbol. It appears within experiments next to steps that require caution. When you see this symbol, ask an adult for help.

Be a safe scientist
Follow all the instructions carefully and always use caution, especially with scissors and sharp objects.

Never put anything in your mouth or eyes. Remember to clean up and put everything away when you have finished each experiment.

Digit dial

How do digital watches, clocks, and calculators display numbers? Find out by making your own digital display.

You will need:

Tape

One large and two small cardboard tubes

Tracing paper

Scissors

Pencil

Felt-tipped pens

Strip of paper

1 Copy this figure onto a small piece of tracing paper. Color everything but the seven segments up to the edges of the "frame" with a black pen.

Color the numbers red.

Trace around the edges of the black rectangle. This is the "frame" for your numbers.

Cut out the window 2 cm (³/₄ in.) from the top of the tube.

2 Trace the figure ten times on the strip of paper. Cut the strip in half. Color the segments that make the numbers 9 to 5 on one half, and 4 to 0 on the other (as shown).

Color the rest of the paper black.

3 ⚠ Ask an adult to cut out a window the same size as the frame from the large cardboard tube.

8

4 Tape the frame inside the large cardboard tube so that it shows through the window.

5 Tape a numbered strip around the top of each of the small cardboard tubes.

6 Insert a small tube inside the large tube. Turn the small tube to see the digits appear one by one. Try the other tube!

Digital watch

A digital watch uses the same kind of frame to display numbers. Each frame is made up of seven segments. The segments that are needed to display a number are darkened by an electric current.

Abacus

Make an adding machine called an abacus. It uses beads to show units of ones, tens, and hundreds. By moving the beads, you can quickly add or subtract numbers from 0 to 999.

You will need:

Shoe box

Tape

Twenty-seven beads (nine each of three colors)

String

Scissors

1 Cut three pieces of string, each one slightly longer than the box.

2 Thread nine beads of the same color onto each piece of string.

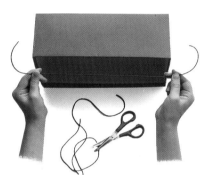

Put the first string in the middle.

3 Stretch a string of beads across the top of the box. Tape the ends of the string to the ends of the box. Do the same with the second string.

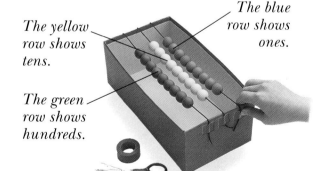

The yellow row shows tens.

The green row shows hundreds.

The blue row shows ones.

4 Add the third string of beads. Push all the beads to one side of the box. This is your abacus.

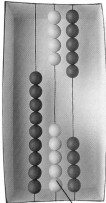

100s 10s 1s

5 First, try counting on your abacus. Move up a ones bead for each number from one to nine. When you reach ten, move down all the ones beads and move up one tens bead, and so on.

This abacus shows 45— no hundreds, four tens, and five ones.

Now the abacus shows three hundreds, two tens, and two ones—322.

100s   10s   1s

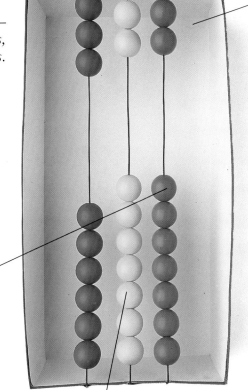

6 Now try some addition. Add 277 to 45. You need to add seven ones, seven tens, and two hundreds to find the answer. Work a few more problems, then try some subtraction.

To add seven, you need to move up seven ones beads. But you have only four left. So move up one tens bead, and then subtract three from the ones column by moving three ones beads down.

Add seven tens in the same way. Then add two hundreds.

Ancient adding machine
The abacus was invented about three thousand years ago, but it is still in use in some parts of the world today, especially in Asia. Expert users can add and subtract quickly on an abacus.

Simple addition

You can make a simple slide rule that will help you with addition. A slide rule is a type of calculator. This one can add any two numbers that total 20 or less—just by sliding a piece of paper.

You will need:

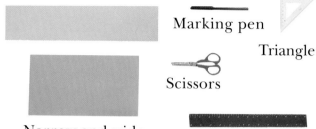

Marking pen

Triangle

Scissors

Narrow and wide pieces of stiff paper

Ruler

Hold the triangle against the ruler to make sure all the lines are straight.

Make the big half as wide as the narrow piece of paper.

1 Fold the wide piece of paper, so that one half is bigger than the other.

2 Using the ruler and triangle, draw twenty-one boxes across both parts of the paper (as shown). Make the lines 1 cm (¹⁄₂ inch) apart.

3 Number the boxes on both sides of the paper from 0 to 20.

4 Insert the narrow piece of paper inside the folded one. Draw eleven more boxes as shown.

5 Number the boxes from 10 to 1 and draw a plus sign in front of each number. Cut out two-thirds of the last box, and write an equals sign in the remaining third.

Here, the slide rule shows 8 + 10 = 18.

The numbers on the two papers are written in the reverse order of each other, one counting up, the other counting down.

Since the boxes are all the same size, any number on the sliding paper will show how many boxes there are between the number on the folded paper and the answer slot.

6 Slip the narrow paper inside the folded one. Slide it up or down to create math problems. The answers to the problems show through the opening.

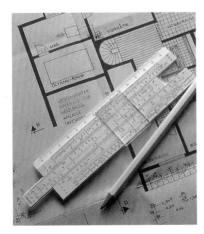

Problem solver
Most slide rules can be used to multiply and divide as well as add and subtract. Before electronic calculators were developed, people used slide rules to solve difficult math problems.

Marble chute

Make a game that keeps score as you play. It shows your score as a "graph." Graphs show numbers in picture form.

You will need:

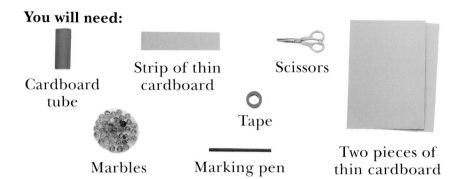

Cardboard tube

Strip of thin cardboard

Scissors

Tape

Marbles

Marking pen

Two pieces of thin cardboard

You should have five gutters.

1 Fold one piece of cardboard into an accordion. Make eleven evenly spaced folds. Then fold the strip of cardboard in half lengthwise.

2 Tape the flat piece of cardboard over one end of the gutters. Tape the folded strip to the other end.

The folded cardboard strip makes a wall at the end of the gutters.

3 Tape the tube near the top of the flat piece of cardboard, in the middle. This is your chute.

4 Number the piece of cardboard that covers the gutters. Place five marbles in an outer gutter. Then write the numbers 1 to 5 up the side of the gutter, in line with the top of each marble.

Number the middle gutter 1, the next two gutters 2, and the outside gutters 3.

5 Set the chute on a pile of books so that it is higher than the gutters. Then try the game. Roll ten marbles down the chute and see your score.

The marbles in the gutters form a graph. By reading the scale on the side, you can tell how many marbles are in each tray, without counting.

The middle gutter scores 1, the next ones score 2, and the outside gutters score 3. Try competing with a friend. The player with the highest score wins.

Facts in pictures
Graphs are a good way to see and understand lots of numbers at the same time. Computers arrange numbers to make graphs like this one.

Snowflake

Many things in nature have what is called a "line of symmetry." If you folded the object along this line, each half would match exactly. Cut several different snowflake shapes—each will be symmetrical but no two will be exactly the same.

You will need:

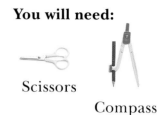

Scissors

Compass

Piece of paper

1 Draw a large circle on the paper with the compass.

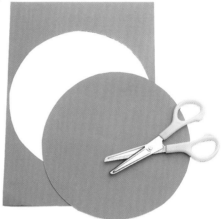

2 Cut out the circle with the scissors.

3 Fold the circle in half. Do not crease the paper too much.

4 Make two more folds in the folded circle, so that it has three equal sections.

Leave space between each notch.

Your snowflake has three lines of symmetry. This means the patterns will match exactly if you fold it along any one of three lines. Refold it and see.

5 Cut a deep notch in the round part of the folded circle. Then cut a few smaller notches in the edges of the circle.

The notch that you cut in the top of the circle is repeated six times.

6 Gently unfold the paper and flatten it out. This is your snowflake.

Each notch that you cut in the edges makes a pattern that is repeated three times.

Natural numbers
These are real snowflakes magnified. Each one is symmetrical. Although two snowflakes of exactly the same shape have never been found, all snowflakes have lines of symmetry.

Number music

You can record your own song using numbers. Make a guitar from a tissue box, then use numbers to write down your music. The numbers let you play your tune again and again.

You will need:

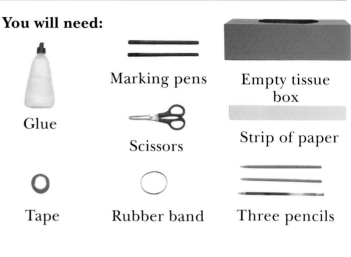

Glue

Marking pens

Empty tissue box

Scissors

Strip of paper

Tape

Rubber band

Three pencils

1 Cut the paper to the same length as the box. Fold it into thirds. Unfold it, and fold it in half. Then fold it into quarters.

Number the folds from right to left.

2 Unfold the paper. Mark and number each fold.

3 Glue the strip of paper along the edge of the box.

This is your instrument's "sound box." It makes the music louder.

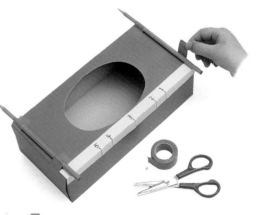

4 Tape a pencil to each end of the box.

5 Stretch the rubber band around the box and over the pencils. It should be taut.

The pencils lift the rubber band off the box, so that you can pluck it.

Pluck the rubber band without using the pencil. Then press the pencil in line with the number 3 and pluck again. You will hear the same note, higher up.

6 Your guitar is ready to play. Press the third pencil onto the rubber band in line with the numbers on the strip, and pluck the rubber band with your finger.

Always pluck the rubber band on the same side of the pencil. How does the sound change as the band gets longer and shorter?

When you have composed a tune that you want to play again, write down the numbers that make it up.

Numbered notes

This computer program can record music as it is played. Each note on the keyboard is given its own number. When someone plays a song, it is stored in the computer's memory as a sequence of numbers that can be played back later.

Weighing machine

We use numbers to tell us exactly how heavy things are. Make a "spring scale" that works by stretching a rubber band. It can tell you the weight of things—but in marbles instead of kilograms or pounds.

You will need:

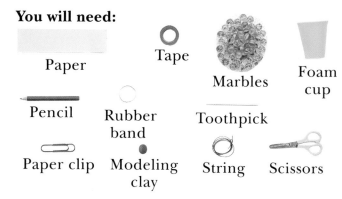

Paper

Tape

Marbles

Foam cup

Pencil

Rubber band

Toothpick

Paper clip

Modeling clay

String

Scissors

1 Cut a short piece of string and tape it to each side of the cup to make a handle.

2 Cut the rubber band and tie one end to the paper clip. Tape the paper clip to a tabletop.

3 Tie the other end of the rubber band to the middle of the handle.

Mark the starting point of the empty cup on the scale.

Make sure all the marbles are the same size.

Add the marbles in twos, each time marking and numbering the scale.

4 ⚠ Push the toothpick through the cup to make a pointer. Cover the point inside the cup with some clay. Tape the paper to the edge of the table to make a scale.

5 Add pairs of marbles to the cup, marking the scale as you go. When you have used all the marbles, empty the cup. You can now use your scale to weigh small objects.

Weighing in
This spring scale weighs objects accurately. It works because the more you pull on a spring, the more it stretches. The amount the spring stretches tells you how much the object weighs.

Counting wheels

How does a counter work? Find out by making your own. You can use it to count from 0 to 99.

You will need:

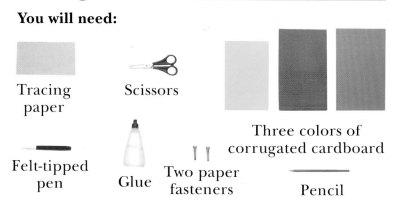

Tracing paper

Scissors

Three colors of corrugated cardboard

Felt-tipped pen

Glue

Two paper fasteners

Pencil

1 Trace the outlines of the two shapes below. Turn the tracing paper over and rub each outline onto a different piece of cardboard.

2 ⚠ Cut out the shapes. Use the pencil to punch holes in the centers.

This is your tens wheel.

Mark the center hole of each shape.

This is your ones wheel.

Write the other numbers from 0 to 9 clockwise on the wheel.

3 Put the ones wheel on top of the tens wheel so that the points match. Draw a 7 on the ones wheel, just below its point.

4 Number the tens wheel counterclockwise from 0 to 9.

Place the wheels side by side so that both wheels stick out slightly over the edge of the cardboard.

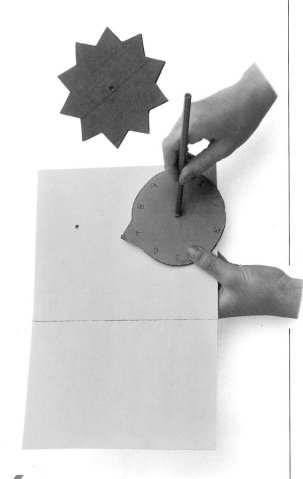

5 Place the two wheels on the third piece of cardboard. Fold it so that all but 2.5 cm (1 in.) of each wheel is covered. Open it again.

6 ⚠ Push the pencil through the hole in each wheel to make a hole in the third piece of cardboard. Remove the wheels.

Make sure both wheels show 0 at the top.

7 ⚠ Fold the cardboard again and turn it over. Then pierce the other side of the cardboard by pushing the pencil through the holes.

8 Cut two triangles from the cardboard scraps to make pointers. Glue the pointers above the holes. Slip the wheels back in place. Push the fasteners through all the holes.

Here the counter shows 19. You can use it to count up to 99.

Keeping count
A car's odometer works in the same way as the counter you have made. The numbers from 0 to 9 are printed on small drums. These drums spin around as the car travels, counting the miles or kilometers.

9 Turn the ones wheel around from 0 to 9. Each time the ones wheel turns from 9 back to 0, the tens wheel moves one notch higher.

How many heartbeats?

Try counting the number of times your heart beats in a minute. Ask a friend to feel your pulse. Your pulse throbs at exactly the same rate as your heart beats.

You will need:

Stopwatch   Jump rope

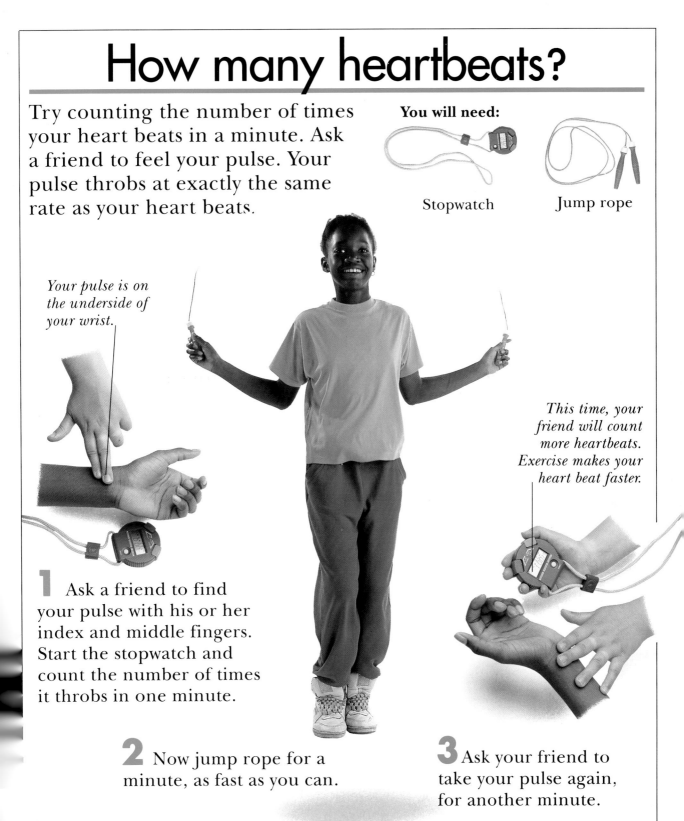

Your pulse is on the underside of your wrist.

This time, your friend will count more heartbeats. Exercise makes your heart beat faster.

1 Ask a friend to find your pulse with his or her index and middle fingers. Start the stopwatch and count the number of times it throbs in one minute.

2 Now jump rope for a minute, as fast as you can.

3 Ask your friend to take your pulse again, for another minute.

Upstairs, downstairs

Move up and down a staircase in this game to find out how numbers show both size and direction. If you start at zero, a "positive" number means move up, a "negative" number means move down, and zero means stay put!

You will need:

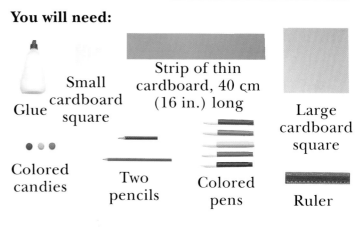

Glue

Small cardboard square

Strip of thin cardboard, 40 cm (16 in.) long

Large cardboard square

Colored candies

Two pencils

Colored pens

Ruler

Number the sections −1, 0, +1, and +2.

1 Use the ruler to draw two diagonal lines from corner to corner of the small cardboard square.

2 Color each section, then push a pencil through the middle of the square, where the lines cross. This is your spinner.

Measure the distance between the folds with the ruler.

3 Fold the strip of cardboard into an accordion by making fifteen folds, each 2.5 cm (1 in.) apart. Unfold the cardboard to make a staircase.

Make sure each step of the staircase is level.

Both positive and negative numbers have value. The sign (+) or (−) shows the direction of each number from zero. So (+3) is three more than zero, and (−3) is three less.

4 Glue the staircase to the large cardboard square as shown. Let the glue dry.

If the spinner lands on 0, do not move your counter. Zero has no value, either positive or negative.

5 Number the stairs from bottom to top, from negative three (−3) to positive three (+3). Number the middle stair zero (0).

6 Play the game with some friends. Start on the middle stair. Take turns spinning the spinner. Move your counter up (+) or down (−) the number of stairs shown on the spinner. The first player to reach the top of the stairs wins.

Below zero

Thermometers use zero and negative numbers. This thermometer shows the temperature in degrees Celsius (°C). Water freezes at zero degrees Celsius. Any temperature below that is shown as a negative number. For example, "minus three" (−3°C) is three degrees below zero.

Shadow clock

You can make a simple clock using shadows and numbers. Shadows change length and direction as the sun moves. The positions of the shadows can show you what time it is.

You will need:

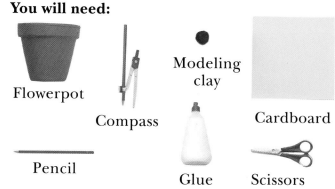

Flowerpot

Compass

Modeling clay

Cardboard

Pencil

Glue

Scissors

1 Draw a large circle on the cardboard with the compass.

2 ⚠ Cut out the circle and make a small hole in its center.

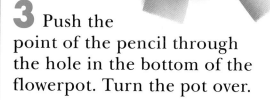

Fix the pencil in place with clay.

3 Push the point of the pencil through the hole in the bottom of the flowerpot. Turn the pot over.

4 Set the circle of cardboard over the pencil and glue it to the bottom of the flowerpot.